SECRETS OF

I0010787

STYLE BLOGGING

The ultimate How-To guide for blogging success

BY: ASHLINA KAPOSTA founder of THE DECORISTA

First published 2012 by Ista Publishing
Updated 2015
Copyright © 2012 Ashlina Kaposta

All rights reserved.

All rights reserved. No part of this publication may be reproduced, distributed, or transmitted in any form or by any means, including photocopying, recording, or other electronic or mechanical methods, without the prior written permission of the publisher, except in the case of brief quotations embodied in critical reviews and certain other noncommercial uses permitted by copyright law. For permission requests, write to the publisher, addressed "Attention: Permissions Coordinator," at the address below.

www.thedecorista.com

Printed in the United States of America

TABLE OF CONTENTS

INTRODUCTION: MY STORY

RESOURCES

THIS BOOK IS DEDICATED TO...
LOUIS J. KAPOSTA,
THE MOST INCREDIBLY TALENTED,
WILDLY ENTHUSIASTIC & EXTREMELY
ENCOURAGING GRANDFATHER A GIRL
COULD HAVE EVER HAD!

Thank you all for reading!

Introduction

Life is beautiful

I've heard people say that if you do what you love, you will end up being successful. In my wildest dreams, I never actually thought that could happen to me. It wasn't until I took a step out of my comfort zone and started a blog, that my dreams have come true. As I find myself staring out of the window gazing upon the beautiful buildings of Manhattan writing this very book, I lean back in my chair, take a deep sigh and realize I am living my wildest dream. This is why I am writing this book, to show you step by step how I found my dreams through blogging and I want to let you know, that you can do it too.

Blogging, the internet and social media have taken my life, my dream, my career, from practically just a cute business card to a full time job and business brand. Upon graduation from college, I set out to Los Angeles to pursue my dreams of being an interior designer. After many failed attempts to land the job of my dreams, I took a job at a real estate development firm in Beverly Hills, learning the ins and out of building a hotel from the ground up. It was a great job, but I was hardly pursuing my passion.

Then, after the big economy crash, our firm shut down and I received the biggest blessing of my life....I was laid off. At the time I had no idea, but getting pushed out of a steady job was actually the beginning of my career.

Shortly after getting laid off, a huge tragedy came upon my life. My grandfather, my hero, was diagnosed with acute Leukemia and passed away in the same week.

I felt like I was punched in the stomach. My whole world stopped making sense. He was the ultimate creative person in my family, and I always admired his ability to pursue his passions. He was a fantastic writer and was always encouraging me to write too. After he passed, I felt deep down in my gut that I needed to start writing. I just had no idea where, when or how but at that moment I just knew that is what I had to do.

Then my boyfriend at the time said to me, "Why don't you start a blog and write about interior design. You love interior design and you want to write. So, do that." The very next day, my blog was born.

When I first started out, I had absolutely no idea what I was doing and just wish that someone had written a book and put it out there for me to learn from. That's why I am writing this book for all of you. So, let's get started!

Chapter 1:

SETTING UP SHOP

CHOOSE A BLOG PLATFORM

....

Luckily, starting a blog can be absolutely free if you want it to. It will be the cheapest business investment you will ever make. There are plenty of options when it comes to free blogging platforms. Most people gravitate towards Blogger or Wordpress. They both are fantastic options with great technology that can basically allow you to customize your blog to look anyway you want. There are several others such as Squarespace, tumblr and Livejournal. The list goes on and on.
Honestly, this decision was way too overwhelming for me.
So let me break it down for you...

When I first started my blog, I wanted the easiest program because I felt extremely intimidated. I could hardly even get around my myspace page. Graphics were so not my specialty and because Blogger goes hand and hand with Gmail, I just went for it.

To my surprise, it was extremely easy and effortless. All of the icons are super self explanatory and the back end is very easy to navigate. Because I was a novice blogger, it was the perfect fit for me. Conversely, after a lot of late nights at my laptop, I was able to teach myself how to navigate the platform so well, that I began to feel like an expert. I was ready to graduate to the next level and I was limited in terms of platform capabilities.

I love Blogger but it only allows you to customize so much, eventually you might feel like you want to do more, which can be very frustrating. If you want to keep your blog on simple side, this platform could be great for you!

I have heard the most amazing things about Wordpress, so after 2 years of being with Blogger, I decided to make the switch to Wordpress. As I mentioned before, Blogger can be
a bit restrictive in terms of your layout and navigation components, where as Wordpress has almost limitless layout configuration and widget capabilities.
Having said that, the backend is a bit more complicated looking and takes some fumbling around to learn your way around the system. There are plenty of templates that are free and if you can find one that you love, you can customize the crap out of it, which is pretty awesome. Now, it's not as pretty and user friendly as Blogger,
but if you aren't afraid of getting in there and teaching yourself a bunch of moves you might love it! I know so many bloggers that do.

Making the switch from Blogger to Wordpress:

For me, making the switch cost me a lot of money and a lot of time. It was not as seamless as I thought it would be. I had to hire someone to design my new site, someone to make the switch and someone to constantly help me make updates and tweaks. To be honest with you, I absolutely hated it. It was so difficult for me to keep everything updated and working in perfect order. I had no idea I had to outsource a host (I used BluHost) which gave me a lot of problems and cost extra money.
This is where you have to decide what it is that you want when it comes to your blog. Do you want versatility & extra functionality (Wordpress) or are you okay with it being easy and basic (Blogger/tumblr)?

SQUARESPACE

My preference is Squarespace. After hearing rave reviews from some friends of mine, I tried Squarespace and honestly, my blog is more beautiful and user friendly than ever. I have a built in host, an easy to add to e-commerce store built right in and a wildly gorgeous template. Everything under one roof and my customization capabilities are pretty wonderful. It took a minute for me to learn but overall was fairly easy. I do pay $20 a month for my blog, which has been cheaper than Wordpress but more than Blogger. To me, its the perfect balance of both. You will have to decide what works best for you and your business but all in all, I am so beyond happy I chose Squarespace.

The best part. It automatically works with everything I need to keep my business running smoothly. Like my newsletters, Youtube videos, etc. I like how everything can work together so seamlessly and look so professional.

As I got more into blogging, I discovered the easiest and most fun blog platform, its called Tumblr. With Tumblr, you can set up your account in seconds and choose from hundreds of gorgeous customized layouts. You wont be able to add tons of great plug-ins and fancy extras like you can with Wordpress and Blogger. However, if you are just using a blog to post photos, send links, or share videos it might be just the platform for you. I have a separate blog on tumblr and it has quickly become my favorite because of the simplicity.

Sometimes they say less is more, no?

My tumblr (decorista daydreams) acts as an addition to my main blog. It's sort of like a fun way to blog images similar to Pinterest boards and bookmark your favorite things. Not many words, just tells your story with images & a vibe.

CHOOSE A DOMAIN NAME

. . . .

Its extremely important to pick a title that you love and don't mind seeing every single day. You want to find something that represents you and your outlook on the subject you are blogging about. I suggest you find a name as soon as possible to avoid confusion later on. When I first started blogging I couldn't really think of a clever name, so I came up with Secretsofdomesticbliss.blogspot.com. For a title, this is way too long of a name for you to consider, trust me. I found it difficult to ever tell anybody or put it on a fabulous business card. After about 6 months of blogging at this name it became clear to me that my blog name was not representing me at all. I wanted something clever and short, to the point, something a little more personal. I also wanted something that would be easy to have across all social media channels under the same name. THE DECORISTA was what my friends would call me, so for me it was perfect.

TO DOT.COM OR NOT?

I also decided that if I wanted to make my blog/website feel a little bit easier to find, I wanted a .com and not a .blogspot.com. A lot of very successful bloggers have kept their blogspot.com and wordpress.com URL and it works great for them. It's all about personal preference, but I did find that having a .com cemented my business and brand. It only costs about 10$ a year and allows you to get more creative with your domain name. A .com is so much easier to fit on things as opposed to .blogspot.com.

DETERMINE YOUR VOICE

It is very, very important to determine what your blog voice will be. You should start by asking yourself a few questions.

Do I want my blog to be more about my personal life or more about my business venture/passions?

Do I want my blog to be anonymous or would I like to showcase my perspective, experiences and knowledge?

Would I prefer my blog to promote me as an individual brand or would I like to promote a business venture?

Each of these questions will get your brain thinking. In my early days of blogging, I had no idea what I wanted to accomplish. I decided to write from my personal perspective about decorating (which later turned into a business), but I didn't make an effort to 'brand' myself. After becoming wildly invested in reading other blogs, I noticed that the blogs I enjoyed the most were the ones that were very personal. I gravitated towards reading those that put up a great headshot, a bio or a personal mission statement. This helped me to feel engaged with the reader and more often than not, those were the ones that I would go back to visit day after day. Whether you blog for business or personal life, having an identity will help you stand out. My advice, don't be afraid to stand out and be different. Putting in a little effort to get creative and brand yourself will pay off in the end.

*CREATING A BIO or MISSION STATEMENT IS
A GREAT WAY TO START OFF WHEN IT
COMES TO FOCUSING ON THE DIRECTION
OF YOUR BLOG AND BRAND!

JEN

A FEW CHOICES:
blogger or wordpress?
blogger
pinterest or tumblr?
haven't had time to play with
either one yet...
facebook or twitter?
hate facebook, love twitter
personal or business only?
depends

MADEBYGIRL.BLOGSPOT.COM

What inspired you to start your blog?

Writing a blog was another means to reach thousands of people who I could inspire as well as introduce my business to. I started my blog back in 2006 and was inspired by the idea of becoming a happy & successful blogger while at the same time inspiring others
to decorate!

How did you find your direction + content?

My content comes mostly from the web itself, although I shoot a lot of my own photos as well. I love home design, in fact im passionate
about it, and that is what i decided to stick to. My direction has always been to do what I want and not always what makes someone else happy.

How often do you post? I post 5-6 times a week....

Do you think its important to comment on other blogs?

Yes, I think it's very important to comment on other blogs. I used to do it more often, but as my blog grew & my business became more successful I found i have less time now. I still try to comment as much as I can on other blogs, because keeping blog relationships can be a win-win. I've noticed that a few bigger name bloggers rarely ever comment on other blogs & it makes them look a bit snobby. I hope I don't ever get to that point....

Do you use photoshop for graphics or are you graphically challenged?

I love photoshop & use it almost everyday...so yes, I use it with graphics.

Was there a moment when you felt an "i made it" moment in terms of your blogs success?

This may sound weird but when i started seeing my Made by Girl link on almost every blog I visited - that was a good feeling. If people were adding me randomly without expecting a reciprocal link, I figured they felt it was a blog worthy of adding to their blogroll!

Is there one particular thing you did that helped your blog succeed?

I dont think there was one thing...but many. I worked 10-12 hours a day on my business & blog when i first started. I didnt have comments on my blog for the first 6 months i think...that sucked. I am not a patient person to begin with so that worried me. Thankfully I kept at it. One thing I know helped my blog was the exchange of links with other blogs.

What would you say is the biggest benefit being a "blogger" has given you?

Free gifts that companies send me...just kidding. Well, Ive never gotten shoes or handbags...darn those fashion bloggers!! They get all the good stuff!. Being that I write about interior design, whose going to send a chair or sofa my way??? Ha! But all kidding aside, one benefit is that I've been able to make my blog a part of my full time business.

Is your blog used to supplement your business or is your blog your business? It's essentially a marketing vehicle for both my Made by Girl & Cocoa & Hearts business..

Any advice for new or novice bloggers....? Don't give up if this is something you really want to do. Also, if you want results, you have to be able & willing to put in the time. Lots of time...

Chapter 2:
MAKING IT PRETTY

DETERMINE THE VIBE

Now that you have set up your blog, you are ready to start decorating it. Of course you want it to look perfect but more importantly, you want it to look like you. I suggest choosing your three favorite blogs that draw your eye and try to gather inspiration from their look. This can help you determine the feel you want your blog to have. Bold and colorful, soft and very simple with small fonts, or fun fonts with big juicy photos. Choose your favorite style and chances are the more you like the look of your blog, the more effort you will put in to it and believe me, your readers will appreciate the effort. I spent 6 months changing up my blog and I even make minor adjustments to this day and I am absolutely in love with it. (I wish I had come up with a fixed plan as to the aesthetics a long time ago, it would have saved me a lot of time.) Like a child, your blog will grow to perfection, it just takes a little time, patience and TLC. Don't get caught up in perfection but...

FIRST IMPRESSIONS ARE EVERYTHING!

Whether you are going to meet your boyfriends' mom for the first time or you are headed to your dream job interview, you want to look your best. The same goes for your blog layout. You want to introduce yourself as pretty, fresh and well put together. You never know who will be reading it.
Let me share with you a few things to keep in mind.

MAKE YOUR HEADER EASILY RECOGNIZABLE
AND BRAND-ABLE, THAT WAY YOU CAN KEEP A COHESIVE
LOOK WHEN GUEST BLOGGING OR ADVERTISING.

A CUTE COLOR STORY

Make sure you stick with a fixed color palate for your blog, and keep in mind that the graphics should tell a story and explain your style. One of my favorite blogs has a very simple header and has one color for all the font. It's easy and basic, and gets the point across. You can be as simple or elaborate as you want. There are so many different blog designs that look fabulous. Again, do your research and see which blog looks you like, this will help lead you in the direction you want to go. Try to not go overboard with graphics in the beginning. You want to make sure that your blog is very user friendly and easy to navigate, because you could potentially deter blog readers if it is too hard to get around.

QUICK COLOR BRAND GUIDE

Green	• calm, soothing, reassurance, peaceful, health, growth, life, healing, money
Blue	• credible, reliable, professional, trust, strength, peace, confidence, integrity
Purple	• curative, protective, thoughtful, wise, imaginative, royal, luxury, dignity
Yellow	• enlightening, abundance, caution, clarity, warmth, optimism, cheerful, friendly
Orange	• energizing, desire, warmth, cheerful, confident
Red	• demanding, passionate, exciting, youthful, danger, daring, urgency
Gray	• balance, neutral, calm, stability, security, strong, character, authority, maturity
Black	• sophistication, power, formality, mystery
White	• freshness, hope, goodness, light, purity, cleanliness, simplicity, coolness
Pink	• romance, compassion, faithfulness, beauty, love, sensitivity
Gold	• wealth, success, status, generous, living, wisdom, charisma, optimistic
Brown	• stable, reliable, approachable, genuine, organic

VISUAL INTEREST

....

Make sure that the images you use are big and powerful, don't get shy on sizing. I will always return to a blog when large photos are very clean and very visible. Fashion bloggers really know how to do this, they post so many yummy and extra large photos I can hardly wait to see them.

It is important to make sure that the post body of your blog is over 600 pixels wide so that images can be large. A good size photo is about 500 pixels wide by 500 pixels tall, at least. In blogger, I learned to manipulate the html and change the size. In most blogging platforms, all you have to do is stretch the photo...easy, peasy.

ALSO, I LOVE THE LOOK OF ALIGNED PHOTOS (WHEN EVERY IMAGE IS THE SAME WIDTH). IT MAKES FOR A REALLY CRISP, CONSISTENT LOOK.

ABOVE THE FOLD

This is the area of the blog that you see before you scroll down the page. It is crucial for any website or blog that this area is the most impactful, as it is likely to determine whether a person continues to stay on your page. Its like the outfit you wear to make a smashing first impression.
It needs to be the best part of the page.
I suggest putting up a photo of yourself in this area if your blog is personal. You will want to have your major links in this area like contact or portfolio. Also, keep in mind this is prime real estate for potential sponsors/advertisers or your subscribe form.

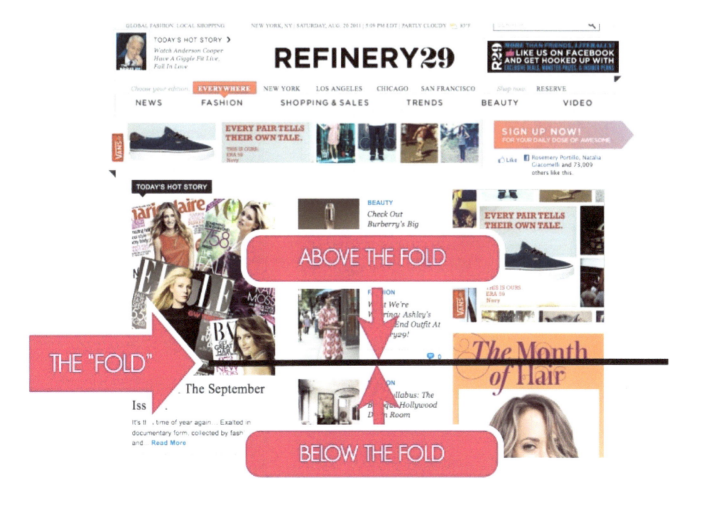

WHEN TO HIRE A BLOG DESIGNER

*If you are challenged in the graphics department and you want your blog to be sharp and stunning.

*If you are planning on using your blog as a platform for your business, you will want to demonstrate your branding properly.

*If you are interested in approaching sponsors, advertisers, and the like you need to ensure that your blog has visual polish.

*When you see another blog with strong visual content and you want your blog to look that good or better, take the leap and hire a graphic designer.

CONSIDER YOUR OPTIONS

Do some blog design research, find a blog layout that you love and find out who the designer is. There is usually a link at the bottom of the blog that will give you the designer's info.

Set a budget in your head and determine what you are willing to spend on blog design. (There is no standard fee and some blog designers can cost several hundred dollars, some several thousand). I don't suggest spending too much money on your blog design at first, mostly because your aesthetic will evolve over time. So, wait and make sure you pay for the look you truly want, don't just rush into it.

Do not be intimidated by expensive blog designers. There is always somebody new and fresh on the scene, who wants to grow their portfolio and will not cost you a fortune. I know several amazing blog designers who charge around 100-500$.

Be sure the person that you hire gets your personality and vision. My advice is to get everything in writing. I cannot tell you how many times I have heard and experienced horror stories about hiring graphic designers who couldn't make deadline or who didn't follow through on promises. Make sure there is a contract and try to get the designer on the phone so you can both have a clear understanding of the terms of the project. You want to be on the same page to ensure proper execution.

WHEN HIRING A GRAPHIC DESIGNER ALWAYS BE SURE TO ASK FOR REFERENCES!

DO IT YOURSELF

If you have no budget for blog design, thats okay. You absolutely can make your blog look fabulous on your own.

START WITH A GREAT HEADER

There are plenty of great places to make a header. Picasa and Photobucket are really great online tools that are free and let you play with images. When I first started out thats how I made my header, I played with tons of different looks and they worked fine. After becoming a more serious blogger, I decided to take the leap and download Photoshop Elements. I am way too intimidated by Photoshop, so I went for the lighter version and have been teaching myself as I go. Its super budget friendly and a great way to get to know graphic design a little better. There are hundreds of online tutorials on you tube as well that can help you learn the way.

In my case, I am pretty obsessed with Apple Pages. I can create great images and headers for my blog and my business. You can also go to places like logoguru.com and hire someone to create your header for you.

CAMILLE

A FEW CHOICES:
blogger or wordpress?
I LOVE wordpress!
pinterest or tumblr?
pinterest
facebook or twitter?
both, but I really prefer twitter
personal or business only?
I use it for personal and business.

CAMILLESTYLES.COM

What inspired you to start your blog?
As an event planner, I'm constantly working with clients who get so overwhelmed and stressed out by parties. I started my blog as a way to show home entertainers how to entertain in a way that's stylish, stress-free and most of all...FUN!

How did you find your direction + content?
Honestly, it took about a year of blogging before I finally determined my focus and voice on my blog. I think that if you're listening to your readers and keeping a close eye on what they're responding to, you'll naturally start to hone in on your blog's unique perspective. For me, the most important thing is to continually push myself to be creative and not settle into too much of a "routine" on the blog.

How often do you post?
Twice daily.

Do you think its important to comment on other blogs?
Commenting is so crucial! The beautiful thing about blogging is that it truly is a community of like-minded people. By engaging in conversation on other people's blogs, you begin to form those relationships and expand your own network. Not to mention the fact that it's just good karma!

Do you use photoshop for graphics or are you graphically challenged?
I majored in advertising in college, and fortunately received a great photoshop education. I now use it daily! But seriously, anyone can learn photoshop. Enroll in a continuing-education photoshop class at a local college, and you'll learn all you need to be a pro.

Was there a moment when you felt an "i made it" moment in terms of your blogs success?
I'm constantly WOW'd by so many amazing moments that have come about as a result of blogging. Being featured on Martha Stewart was pretty cool as was an LA Times piece that just came out. If you believe in what you're doing, the sky really is the limit!

Is there one particular thing you did that helped your blog succeed?
Persistence. Every blogger has that moment when they want to give up, because you wonder if it's worth it/if anyone is reading/ how you can possibly find the time to keep going. But if you truly love blogging, hang in there! Create great content and the readers will follow, I promise.

What would you say is the biggest benefit being a "blogger" has given you?
Without a doubt, the great friendships that I've made all over the country. I had no idea what an amazing community of creative people were out there, and I often laugh because I communicate more frequently with my "blog friends" than my friends who live in the same town! Thank goodness for Twitter for keeping in touch.

Is your blog used to supplement your business or is your blog your business?
It started as a way to support my event planning business, but as it's grown, my blog has become the main focus of my company.

Any advice for new or novice bloggers....?
Consider ways to start living your dream where you are right now. If you really want to be a blogger, then there's no time like the present! Never forget that life is way too short to waste one day working in a role that's uninspiring. You'll always regret it if you don't give your dream a shot, so go for it!

Chapter 3:
GIVING GOOD CONTENT

YOU GET WHAT YOU GIVE

Now that your blog is up and running and looking fabulous, we have got to talk about the MOST IMPORTANT aspect of your blog...content. When you have established the voice, direction and look of your blog, you can be more clear in terms of what your content will be.

DILIGENT EFFORT

=

GOOD CONTENT

=

SUCCESS

I can tell you from experience that creating great content can take hours upon hours of effort. I spent so many late nights on my laptop searching for new things and keeping myself up to date on all information related to decorating. I knew that in order for me to have a good blog, I would need to give a lot of effort into the research and development for good content to give to my readers. Even if you think no one is reading your blog, you must know that somebody out there is going to see it, so write like you have millions reading.

SUBSCRIBE TO EVERY MAGAZINE AND ONLINE NEWSLETTER IN YOUR RELATED FIELD SO THAT YOU CAN CONSTANTLY GET INSPIRED FOR NEW BLOG POSTS.

THE KEY IS CONSISTENCY

When I ask successful bloggers their secrets to success, one word sticks out the most and that is; consistency. When formulating your voice you can make some concise decisions that will help you to keep your content consistent. Making sure to be deliberate in your efforts and consistent with your content is a sure way to solidify your professionalism. So try to determine your blogging style and stick with it.

You can start by making a few crucial decisions such as, will your posts be centered or right aligned? You should take into consideration each of the little details about your post, font size, image size, how much font, how many photos, how often you post, what types of posts, etc. In my case, I knew that I didn't really like to read magazine articles because I have visual ADD, I just love pretty pictures. So, I decided that I would keep my text very short and only add a few lines of my voice. I wanted to let the vibe of my post be conveyed through beautiful imagery. I decided early on that I didn't want to blog like anyone else. I wanted to make my blog mostly for me, so I created a blog mold that fit what I would love to read. I banked on the fact that if I loved it, then surely someone out there would love it too. Chances are, if you do that for your own blog, there will be more people out there that like what you like than you realize.

Something to keep in mind...

Blogging should never be taken too seriously. It's a journey that you embark on and patience for the process is highly encouraged. While it's important to treat your blog in a professional manner, it's important to go with the flow. Understand that most people who start a blog end up writing about something totally different than they began with. It happens to the best of us. I started out writing about random things I liked in home decor, lifestyle and fashion, my posts were all over the place and very light on text. As I continued to write blog posts day after day, I slowly started to get a more clear vision about my blog voice (the direction in which my blog message was headed). That's when I was able to write more, I had a better idea of what I wanted to say and how I wanted to say it.

After hearing feedback from readers and commenters, I was able to refine my content and create a direction more focused on interiors because thats what I truly love the most and what others loved too. So, I learned to write about how to decorate and very clear reasons why decorating can be fun. Decorating is the main topic of my blog and how to create domestic bliss through decoration is my specific niche. When I do write about off topic things such as fashion, it always relates to design and decorating.

After the last few years, I also blog a lot about business advice. It's part of my blog evolution and I love to be open and share what inspires me. Now being an *entrepreneuress* inspires me just as much as decorating does.

Enjoy the process of finding your niche and be comfortable exploring a direction you may not think will work at first. Eventually, you will come to find what you enjoy blogging about and what you feel most confident with. It may take you some time, but it will come, I promise.

BUILDING A LIST

One of the most important aspects of growing your blog and/or your brand is a healthy subscriber list. Let's face it, not everyone is going to have time to remember to read all of their favorite blogs everyday. I certainly can't. This is why you should have a newsletter or email subscribe sign up form on the main page of your blog. Having a newsletter list is a great way to keep in front of your blog readers and remind them of you. You can send your top 3 most recent blog posts every week or even every month if you wish. A newsletter list also helps to keep a consistent flow of traffic to your blog. It keeps you fresh in your blog readers mind so they will check back in again and again.

Also, if you plan to launch products, offer sales or new business services, your email list will be a great way for you to communicate that to your readers. Make sure you start building your list early on. I waited way to late in the game.

I personally use a service called MailChimp. They are free for a certain amount of emails and super easy to navigate. However, there are many fantastic newsletter list builders out there for you to use.

IT IS BEST TO KEEP NEWSLETTER CONTENT DIFFERENT THAN YOUR BLOG CONTENT. THIS ENGAGES READERS IN A FRESH WAY AND DELIVERS A LOT OF VARIETY TO KEEP THEM COMING BACK FOR MORE.

A FEW CONTENT IDEAS

....

START A SERIES:

Perhaps you want to start something like 'fashionista fridays' or 'thoughts on thursday'. Be creative in a weekly or monthly series concept.

TELL A STORY:

I always think sharing a personal story or experience is a great way to get connected with readers.

REVIEW A PRODUCT:

Talk about your favorite beauty secret, a new restaurant you have tried out or even a book you recently read. People love feedback and more information.

CONDUCT A SURVEY OR ASK QUESTIONS:

One time I needed to know what people thought about what wall color to paint. This was a great way to get engaged with my readers and hear from them. This also helps inspire new content.

INTERVIEWS & RAVE REVIEWS:

A great idea is to find another blogger you admire, ask them some questions and give them a glowing review. This is a great way to get connected + expand your blog.

BUILD BLOGGER RELATIONSHIPS

After years of blogging I can honestly say that having a network and friendships that I have built through blogging is the aspect that has given me the most joy. Aside from being part of an extremely supportive community, I have created friendships with people who have similar interests. I have made some of my best friends through blogging and they are the kind of relationships built on camaraderie, which is unlike any other friendship. As you venture on your blogging journey, I suggest you begin by getting out there and making friends. It will help you to grow a lot faster than just going into this on your own.

You can comment on your favorite blogs, attend workshops and even host meet ups in your own city. It's highly rewarding.

WILL

A FEW CHOICES:
blogger or wordpress?
Blogger
pinterest or tumblr?
Pinterest all the way!
facebook or twitter?
Twitter
personal or business only?
Either, whatever
works for the author

WWW.BRIGHTBAZAARBLOG.COM

WHAT INSPIRED YOU TO START YOUR BLOG?
I FELT CREATIVELY FRUSTRATED AND NEEDED A SPACE TO DOCUMENT MY INSPIRATIONS, SO BRIGHT.BAZAAR WAS BORN. BY A WONDERFUL TURN OF EVENTS IT TURNED OUT TO BE A GREAT PLATFORM FOR MEETING LIKE-MINDED INDIVIDUALS WHO SHARE MY LOVE FOR GREAT DESIGN AND I'VE NOT LOOKED BACK SINCE.

HOW DID YOU FIND YOUR DIRECTION + CONTENT?
HAVING ALWAYS HELD A COLOURFUL AESTHETIC FROM THE BRIGHT YELLOW RUCKSACK I HAD WHEN I WAS A KID TO THE BOLD AND BRIGHT COLOURS I USE IN MY HOME NOW, IT FELT NATURAL TO FOCUS ON MY LOVE OF ALL THINGS COLOURFUL IN INTERIORS AND STYLING.

HOW OFTEN DO YOU POST?
AT LEAST SEVEN DAYS A WEEK, SOMETIMES MORE.

DO YOU THINK ITS IMPORTANT TO COMMENT ON OTHER BLOGS?
PERSONALLY I REALLY LIKE TO COMMENT ON POSTS I READ, ESPECIALLY IF THEY REALLY RESONATE WITH ME OR I FEEL I HAVE SOMETHING I CAN ADD TO THE DISCUSSION - LIKE A HINT OR A TIP FOR A CERTAIN IDEA/PROJECT. THAT BEING SAID, I DON'T HAVE THE TIME TO COMMENT ON AS MANY POSTS AS I WOULD LIKE.

DO YOU USE PHOTOSHOP FOR GRAPHICS OR ARE YOU GRAPHICALLY CHALLENGED?
WHILST I WAS AT UNIVERSITY I DID A FEW INTERNSHIPS IN ART DEPARTMENTS OF TWO PUBLISHING HOUSES SO I PICKED UP SOME GRAPHICS KNOWLEDGE THERE AND TRY TO PUT IT INTO USE IN MY POSTS.

WAS THERE A MOMENT WHEN YOU FELT AN "I MADE IT" MOMENT IN TERMS OF YOUR BLOGS SUCCESS?
BEING FEATURED IN MAGAZINES IN AMERICA, BRITAIN, AUSTRALIA, ITALY AND SINGAPORE HAVE ALL MADE THE HARD WORK I PUT INTO THE SITE WORTHWHILE, BUT ULTIMATELY IT'S THE PLEASURE I GET FROM SHARING MY INSPIRATIONS EACH DAY AND HEARING WHAT INSPIRES OTHERS THAT I LOVE THE MOST.

IS THERE ONE PARTICULAR THING YOU DID THAT HELPED YOUR BLOG SUCCEED?
CONSISTENCY IS THE KEY I THINK: CHOOSE A TOPIC OR SERIES OF TOPICS YOU ARE TRULY PASSIONATE ABOUT AND YOUR VOICE WILL NATURALLY SHINE THROUGH. ALSO, THERE IS NO RIGHT OR WRONG ABOUT HOW OFTEN YOU SHOULD POST. I THINK THE BEST THING TO DO IS TO PICK A POSTING SCHEDULE THAT WORKS FOR YOU AND THEN STICK TO IT SO YOUR READERS BECOME FAMILIAR WITH IT.

WHAT WOULD YOU SAY IS THE BIGGEST BENEFIT BEING A "BLOGGER" HAS GIVEN YOU?
DEFINITELY ALL THE WONDERFUL AND INSPIRING PEOPLE I HAVE MET. SINCE STARTING BLOGGING I'VE MADE SO MANY NEW FRIENDS AND EVEN TRAVELLED TO VISIT SOME OF THEM IN OTHER COUNTRIES.

IS YOUR BLOG USED TO SUPPLEMENT YOUR BUSINESS OR IS YOUR BLOG YOUR BUSINESS?
I DO SHARE MY STYLING PROJECTS ON THE BLOG BUT SEE IT MORE AS A SEPARATE ENTITY - A HOBBY IF YOU LIKE.

ANY ADVICE FOR NEW OR NOVICE BLOGGERS....?
AS I TOUCHED ON BEFORE, I THINK BEING CONSISTENT IS ONE OF THE BEST ASSETS TO ANY BLOGGER.

Chapter 4:

SCHMOOZE OR YOU LOSE

COMMENTS ARE A GIRLS BEST FRIEND

Commenting is a surefire way to start making blog friends. Visit various blogs frequently and make comments on posts that you like and have a positive comment for. When leaving a comment, keep in mind the old adage 'if you don't have anything nice to say, don't say anything at all', nobody likes a sour apple.

It's best to develop a common ground with bloggers, so if you find the post interesting, feel free to say something that shows that you are in agreement on the topic. I suggest finding a few blogs that are in a similar niche and have been blogging around the same length of time. If you are just starting out your blog, find some that are fairly new as well. Once you become friends, you will have so much to discuss and you can give each other great feedback and help each other grow along the way.

To this day I still talk to my first blog friends, we ended up becoming close, personal friends and have encouraged each other to grow to success.

MY 2 RULES TO REMEMBER:

1-DON'T BE SHY. EVERYBODY LOVES TO MAKE A NEW FRIEND. KIND WORDS ARE HIGHLY EFFECTIVE.

2-THE BLOG WORLD IS A SUPER SUPPORTIVE COMMUNITY. ACT ACCORDINGLY!

GO AHEAD, SEND AN E-MAIL

Once you feel you have opened the lines of communication via commenting, twitter, etc, feel free to send over an email introducing yourself. Showing your appreciation and interest in the blog goes a long way. Then feel free to ask questions or to communicate what you want.

Treat every blogger as you would like to be treated, wouldn't you love to hear some positive feedback on your efforts? More often than not, they will be delighted to hear from you and will return the favor.

However, if you send out an email and don't hear back, don't take it personally. Sometimes, other bloggers have full time jobs and barely have time to blog, let alone respond to emails. I have a hard time doing it myself. Blog friendships should organically grow, you will find the right people and the friendship should develop naturally. Don't feel the need to over exert yourself in making friends, it will happen with time.

THIS IS HOW WE BLOG-ROLL

Creating an area on your blog for links to your favorite blogs is a great way to showcase your support. It's so nice to visit another blog and see a link to your own blog. It's one of the biggest and best compliments you could get.

When I first started out, I sent emails to other bloggers in my niche and politely suggested that we exchange links. Why not? It's a great way to get your blog noticed and if they say no, put up their blog anyway. You never know if in the future they will return the favor.

On that same note, if you see your blog on someone else's blog roll, its such a great gesture to add them on yours.

GUEST POST GOODNESS

A great way to get community involvement in your blog is to start a guest posting series or somehow incorporating featuring other blogs into your content. I started a series called SIX TO BLISS, where I asked some of my favorite bloggers to share their personal secrets to domestic bliss. It worked famously, not only did I get to know my fellow bloggers better, it opened up a line of communication between us. It can be such a mutually beneficial concept because it introduces your readers to their blog and potentially will also introduce their readers to you! It's a great way to expand your blog network and get you some extra traffic flow. Before you start something like this make sure your blog is full of great content and your aesthetic vision can come across easily, you want to make sure to captivate new readers.

WHO TO ASK

When you start a series, make sure to have it be in relation to the content of your blog. For example, don't ask guest posts to be about their favorite movie, if your blog is about fashion. Why would your readers want to know about a strangers take on movies, when they are accustomed to seeing fabulous fashion posts. If you want to add a movie flair, relate it to fashion by asking their favorite film based on the costumes. Use your common sense with this and try to make it interesting and relatable. Ask bloggers who you think have something interesting to say and you would genuinely be interested in their answer.

HOW TO ASK

Compose a very complimentary and encouraging email when you invite them to do a guest post. It is mutually beneficial but it does take time for them to put something together, so be appreciative. I also suggest sending a follow up thank you card in the mail. Bloggers love getting things in the mail. Keep a great rapport with bloggers and its likely that the favor will be returned.

GET SOCIAL

If you are fortunate enough to live in a city where there are blog events I strongly encourage you to attend. You never know who you could potentially meet. I attended a seminar on blogging early in my blogging days and I met my future bosses and soon after I landed the job of my dreams. Networking in your blog niche in person will be invaluable to your success as a blogger. Not only will you meet people with similar interests, you could learn tricks of the trade and the do's and dont's of blogging.

BE A HOSTESS WITH THE MOSTEST

Now that the world of blogging has grown so popular, it is likely that someone will host a meet up in your city. When I started my blog I was in LA and fortunately there were several events to attend. However, a lot of them were fashion related so I took it upon myself to organize a design blogger dinner, in fact, I did a few of them. Some were successful and some were not but I had a great time even if I only got to meet a few. This was a crucial part of blogging for me, I learned so much just by asking questions and sharing my experiences with my counterparts.

PALOMA

A FEW CHOICES:
blogger or wordpress?
Blogger, but I use Windows Live Writer to write and format my posts, so I don't actually use the Blogger interface. Live Writer is the best blogging tool and I can't imagine using anything else. Live Writer and Hypersnap are essential for new bloggers!
pinterest or tumblr?
Pinterest...I am beyond obsessed!
facebook or twitter?...
I use both. My accounts are linked, so my tweets post to my Facebook page.
personal or business only?
Personal, for sure. I think the best and most successful blogs are those that are personal and engaging.

WWW.LADOLCEVITABLOG.COM

What inspired you to start your blog?
I started La Dolce Vita back in July of 2007 while I was still a high school Spanish teacher. It was summer and I was bored and in need of a creative outlet. I started out writing personal essays about random subjects including interior design which then became the main focus my blog. Over the years, it's grown to be a lifestyle destination rooted in interior design, fashion, travel and living a stylish life.

How did you find your direction + content?
Content and inspiration can be found just about anywhere from a cocktail party to a trip to an exciting, new city. You just have to approach life with an open mind and an eager set of eyes ready to soak up some inspiration.I try to be as focused and organized as possible, which is probably my Type-A personality shining through. I create a calendar every week for the posts and topics I plan to cover that week. I also keep a running list of topics that I want to explore. Sometimes, I dive right in and blog about them immediately. Other times, it may take me a month before I post about that topic. I started running different series on La Dolce Vita with the inception of "10 Things I Can't Live Without" in the fall of 2009 in which I invited inspiring bloggers to share their favorite things with my readers. Since then, I've developed a few other series including "The Style Files", "Fabulous Room Friday" and "Dream Home". Not only is it interesting to see different blogger's perspectives on the same topics, it also gives the blog a sense of continuity and clear focus. Just like with a magazine, my readers know that each week, they'll be able to read regular features mixed in with a few surprises. Every week starts with "This Week's Quote", ends with "Fabulous Room Friday" and has a few unexpected and exciting topics everyday in between.

How often do you post?
I post one or two times daily, Monday through Friday. When I first started writing my blog four years ago, I would just post whenever I thought of something new, maybe three times per week. I quickly learned how important it was to provide consistent, exciting material, especially for new bloggers trying to grow their readership. In 2010, I set a goal to post twice a day, every day, except for Fridays and saw significant growth as a result. I have to admit, it isn't easy coming up with fresh content that hasn't already been blogged to death 9-10 per week.

Do you think its important to comment on other blogs?
Absolutely! Blogging is about community more than anything else. In order to be a part of that community, you have to get out there, show support, and interact with other bloggers. I wish I had the time to comment on my favorite blogs more often, but sadly I can't do so as often as I'd like. If you're a new blogger, this is probably one of the most crucial elements in getting your name out there, building a readership, and establishing relationships within your blogging community.

Do you use photoshop for graphics or are you graphically challenged?
Sadly, I am graphically challenged and don't know Photoshop or InDesign. I desperately want to take a Photoshop course when I have the time. It is on the top of my list of blogging goals!

Was there a moment when you felt an "i made it" moment in terms of your blogs success?
It was when I received my first, big press mention. I was the "Blogger to_____" in Better Homes and Gardens. I remember how surreal it was to see my face looking back at me in the magazine while I was in the supermarket check out aisle. More than anything, it was crazy to think that people were actually reading my blog!

Is there one particular thing you did that helped your blog succeed?
I've always tried to be as genuine as possible. I think my true voice and personality come through in my blog. I've also chosen to keep the mood positive. Sure, there are interiors that I find hideous and red carpet looks that I am less than crazy about, but I choose to focus on the positive rather than tear people down. I firmly believe that if you don't have anything nice to say, it's better not to say anything at all. I think that being honest and approachable as well as supportive and enthusiastic of fellow bloggers along with posting inspiring content that I know my readers will love on a regular basis have all been major factors in making my blog "successful". I look at my readership stats every now and then, and while I know the numbers, it is still surreal to think that people are out there reading and hopefully enjoying the things that I blog about.

Is your blog used to supplement your business or is your blog your business?
My blog isn't necessarily my business per se, but it has facilitated a lot of the other things that I have done like freelance writing, social media consultancy and of course, High Gloss Magazine. These opportunities have all been made possible for me because of my blog. I made the decision to accept sponsors in February of 2009, so I do have some monetary compensation from writing La Dolce Vita, but more than anything, it has opened the doors for other opportunities including a new one that I am currently working on.

Any advice for new or novice bloggers...?
Aside from some of the other things I mentioned earlier, I would say the following things are imperative:
 -Have a Clear Focus
-Write about Original, Engaging Content- There's no sense in blogging about something that has already appeared on 20 blogs unless you have an original take on it.
- Consistency is Key- Whether you choose to post 3 times per week or 10 times per week, be consistent. You can't go weeks without blogging and expect that people will be there to read what you have to say when you get back.
-Make your Blog Attractive and Easy to Read
-Comment on Other Blogs and Network as Much as Possible
-Have Fun! Blogging can be very time consuming, so make sure your heart is in it for the right reasons. I wouldn't still be doing this after four years if I didn't absolutely love it.

Chapter 5:
SOCIAL-MEDIA-IZING

SOCIAL-IZE YOURSELF

Oh, the joys of social networking and social media. I can't imagine what life would be like without Facebook, Twitter, Pinterest, etc. They have become such an integral part of my world. I depend on social media not only for personal use but especially for my business. Before I started blogging, I wasn't too familiar with all of the components that social media has to offer but once I dove into the world I realized how incredibly beneficial it can be. I suggest you take full advantage of what's out there. It can revolutionize your blog and/or your business.

facebook

FAN PAGE + LIKE BUTTON

From your personal Facebook account you can create a business page or a fan page, which I highly suggest. From here you can link your blog to regularly update your page with posts through NetworkedBlogs. This will also allow people on facebook to see your blog if they aren't regular blog readers. It also keeps friends and family up to date on your blog happenings. You can really build a community on your Facebook page too, I have found this extremely beneficial in my business.

THINGS YOU CAN DO WITH FACEBOOK:

~POST FREQUENT STATUS UPDATES
~ENGAGE WITH YOUR READERS VIA COMMENTS
~POST POLL QUESTIONS TO GET FEEDBACK
~POST PHOTOS RELEVANT TO YOUR SITE

THE POWER OF TWITTER

Most people I know are still confused by twitter and can't quite wrap their head around it. I must tell you though, Twitter is one of the most powerful social media platforms out there and can do amazing things for exposure of your site and business.

Once you sign up and get the hang of it, it's really pretty simple. You can carry on conversations and build relationships seamlessly through Twitter. Reading updates of my favorite brands and businesses keeps me ahead of the curve and up to date on whats new and fresh on the scene.

Make sure to follow all brands and businesses in your niche and connect virtually.

If you want to attract more followers quickly, post updates a few times a day with very relevant links, photos and information that will be interesting to people in your field. Also, never be shy of re-tweeting other businesses posts as well. They will love you for it and probably follow you too!

TIP: #HASHTAGS WORK! WHEN YOU WANT TO INCLUDE YOUR TWEETS IN A CATEGORY USE A #. FOR EXAMPLE #FASHIONISTA...OR SOMETIMES I DO #ASHLINAKINTERIORS

Now this is the newest girl on the scene but quickly becoming one of the biggest. It's really meant for connecting business professionals and for acquiring new talent or employment. Even if you feel that you aren't really blogging for business, I strongly encourage you to join. Any and all social media can be good for you. Treat your blog like a business, even if you don't feel that is your direction you never know what possibilities or opportunities will find you.

NAVIGATING LINKEDIN

1. Complete Your Profile
2. Increase Your Connections
3. Customize Your Website Links

4. Update Status
5. Join Niche Groups
6. Post Comments In Groups
7. Add the Blog Application to Your Profile

THE POWER OF PINTEREST

I can't explain the importance of having a pinterest account for your blog and business. It is one of the best tools for getting traffic to your blog. As much fun as it is to just spend hour perusing your feed, I'm going to explain a few Pinterest strategies that will be so helpful to grow your blog.

1. Organization: Keep your boards, especially your top 5 boards in a consistent theme. If you are a fashion gal, have your best photo boards up first. If you are a wedding planner, have your portfolio at the top, your inspirations next, your tips and resources next...you get the idea.

2. Infographics: Create pretty images with your blog titles on top of your image. This engages pinners to click and share your pin more than just images. This lets them know exactly what they are getting and helps to spread your content like wildfire. (Example: 3 ways to make a sandwich for beginners)

3. Freqency: Keep pinning and pinning. The more you pin, the more people will get to see your aesthetic and your brand. There are some apps out there where you can set up and schedule your pins to go out throughout the day. The more you are active and engaging on Pinterest, the more followers you will get. That will bring more readers to your blog.

4. Links: If you are pinning from your blog or your business, make sure the links go directly to the image or product you want to push. Sometimes links don't work so check them often.

5. Hashtags + Keywords: In the description area use hashtags and searchable words so they your photos will come up higher when people are searching for images.

THE MORE THE MERRIER

When it comes to social media, there are hundreds of websites that connect people in the blog world that I have not mentioned. I suggest you get online and do your research. There are plenty of other sites that your favorite bloggers probably belong to. I love Bloglovin', BlogHer, StumbleUpon, Tumblr, Pinterest, Bloggers.com, Blogrankings among so many others. Getting links to your blog out there can help you get your blog noticed and is extremely crucial to Google spider crawlings (more on that in a later chapter).

HOW TO MAKE THEM WORK FOR YOU...

If you are already signed up in various social media outlets then you are on the right path. However, you could be signed up for all of them but still not see that much traffic on your blog.

A few key things to do to increase traffic...

-Make sure all outlets link back to your blog homepage. You want to make sure all sources will take everyone directly to your home page.

-Ensure your RSS feed streams to each social media outlet. In other words, make sure that all of your pages automatically update each time you create a new post. So, if you frequently post, you will keep at the top of the social media feeds.

-Connect with everyone in your niche and beyond. Make sure to friend everyone, follow their feeds, link up with them. Like other pages, tweet people back. Make a continuous effort to socialize online, go above and beyond.

-Put up a headshot on each profile or a consistent branded image so that you will be recognizable and familiar to other members.
Trust me, the more recognized + plugged in you are the better.

REBECCA

REBECCA

A FEW CHOICES:
blogger or wordpress?
Wordpress. I personally don't use it bc I started with
Blogger but am considering changing soon.
pinterest or tumblr?
Pinterest 100%
facebook or twitter?
Hmmm, both.
personal or business only?
also both. My blog, loving, living, small., is a personal blog
but I am able to share some of my professional work
and writing on there as well. It's good to infuse
both into your blog.

LOVINGLIVINGSMALL.COM

What inspired you to start your blog?
I started my blog in early 2008, after moving back from New York a year earlier. I had lived in a super small studio in Soho that I just loved! I was flipping through some old photos of my time in NY and was inspired to start the blog so I could also write about what I loved so much about that apartment. And since it was only 300 square feet, I decided to name it loving. living. small. and to write about my love of design and making a (small) house a home. It really began as an online journal and still is to this day.

How did you find your direction + content?
I knew that I wanted to talk about living in small spaces under 1000 sq feet in both form and function - kind of a look good and feel good style. This is still the foundation of loving. living. small., it's a lifestyle blog for me to document what makes me smile and what I love in regards to my home. As far as content, It's funny looking back, I actually started posting a ton of original content right away. I pulled ideas from my own photo collection. I also started reading other design blogs and connecting with the bloggers. At that time, the community was a lot smaller but still as awesome as it is today. I loved to link to people and share the love. Over the last few years, I started more original series that were born out of things I personally wanted to know about or things I wanted to read - A SMALL CHAT is an interview series that highlights designers, bloggers and design lovers, SMALL SPACE DWELLERS is when I take a real person's room and give small space tips pulled from the design, A SMALL MOVE is based on my own move back to Los Angeles last summer and how I set-up my small space, SMALL SPACE DIY feature cool and affordable projects for your small space that you can do in your own home and more.

Was there a moment when you felt an "i made it" moment in terms of your blogs success?
My first "wow people are reading this" is when I got my first comment a week after I started my blog. And it wasn't from my mom. :) I would say I've had 2 big "I made it" moments. The first was when Apartment Therapy LA posted about my blog on their site a few months after I had started it. Interestingly enough, a few weeks after that, the ATLA team was looking for a new blogger and I submitted my work and was picked to be an LA contributor. I wrote for them for two years. The 2nd big "I made it" moment was last November when InStyle magazine picked my little blog as one of their five BEST OF WEB 2010 home blogs. It was totally surreal and crazy but I felt honored to be part of such a fantastic group of bloggers.

Is there one particular thing you did that helped your blog succeed?
I think small details make a big impact. I use Blogger and taught myself how to alter the template that I was using. I took off the photo borders, I changed fonts, colors and learned how to add sidebar images and my own header, etc. Even my photos have a little detail - I round every picture in photoshop before I post it. It keeps the blog looking clean and cohesive which makes for fluid and easy reading.

Any advice for new or novice bloggers....?
1) If you haven't started a blog and want to - go for it! You can jump in anytime, share your personality on your blog, connect with new friends and more. And try not to feel overwhelmed by other blogs or sites that have tons and tons of readers. Your blog is unique and has a perspective and people will read it, I promise.

2) I would definitely pick your "persona" before your start. For example, I decided to go by "loving. living. small" instead of Rebecca on my blog. I also decided not to really share too many personal things. For me, that's what made sense. I think this is important for business owners - are you your name or your shop's name? Do you want to share, for example, that you just got married or keep that more private? Either way is fine, just stay consistent. And speaking of consistency, create an editorial schedule for you and for your readers in regards to your posts. Maybe Mondays you do a post about your business, Wednesdays you do a post about something that inspired you and Fridays you do a roundup post. A schedule will help you get your posts written and up on your blog.

3) Definitely say hello and connect to bloggers that you love reading. But don't leave this in the comment section. Send a personal email to them and just say "hi, love your blog", etc. Almost every blogger has a contact on their blog.

4) Attend offline events and/or conferences. While we are online a lot, most of us crave to meet up in person and get to know each other and start new friendships.

Chapter 6:
THE POWER OF SEO

THE 'DOWN-LO' ON S.E.O

Its really important for you to understand the web and search engines if you want your blog to soar to the top. If you can harness the power of Google and all that it has to offer, this can help you be a web success. Most people are intimidated by the phrase 'search engine optimization' and I am here to tell you that you need not to be. Allow me to break this down for you and tell you the only things you REALLY need to know.

SEARCH ENGINE OPTIMIZATION:

is the process of improving the visibility of a website or a web page in search engines via the "natural" or un-paid search results. In general, the earlier (or higher on the page), and more frequently a site appears in the search results list, the more visitors it will receive from the search engine's users.

....

You want to improve your SEO rank constantly, this will keep your traffic numbers high and make sure you are more visible to people who randomly search the net!

....

THIS IS ESPECIALLY TRUE WITH GOOGLE IMAGES. ONE TIME I HAD A FREIND WHO SEARCHED THE WORD FABULOUS AND A PICTURE OF ME POPPED UP ON PAGE 2. THAT'S THE POWER OF SEO!

"So, how do i improve my SEO?"

FIRST, You must understand the 3 components Google 'spider crawlers' use to search the web.

TEXT ANALYSIS

Not only does Google look for matching words on a webpage, it also looks for how those words are used. Font size, italics, bold, proximity to similar words, among many others are all factors in determining your 'searchability'. Make sure to place key words in your posts that are relevant to the post. For example, if your post is about "red stilettos', make sure those exact words are included, not only in the post but in the labels as well.

LINKS AND LINK TEXT

Google wants to make sure that the links within your posts are relevant to your content. So make sure to link to any all companies and websites that have similar content. It will consider you a hub for good information.

PAGE RANK

There are several factors that determine your Page Rank but the most important that I know of are Link Backs. In other words, the more other websites and blogs link to your site, the higher your page rank. It's totally like high school, the more popular you are, the higher your rank. This goes hand in hand with me suggesting to you in a previous chapter that its important to exchange links with other bloggers. It does wonders for your Google popularity!

a few things to know...

-Social media sites you will let you place a link to your site, which is great for your Google Page Rank. So the more social media sites you are linked up to the better!

-Images are NOT SEO friends. It's actually text that grabs the attention of Google's spiders. So, if you prefer to use graphics with pretty fonts instead of standard text, make sure to use up your tags and labels with proper key words to ensure your attractiveness to Google.

THE BOTTOM LINE:

Take note of these factors and watch your Google Rank soar to new heights.

CARA

A FEW CHOICES:
blogger or wordpress?
blogger
pinterest or tumblr?
pinterest
facebook or twitter?
facebook
personal or business only?
a gentle mix of both

WWW.THECHAMPAGNEDIET.COM

What inspired you to start your blog?

Quite literally, a glass of champagne. In 2008, I had a moment while working at my (then) day job at MTV. I turned to a coworker and told her I was going on a new diet and she started questioning me, asking for all the details. She was so fed up with me constantly trying all these fad diets that never worked and she begged me to just eat whole, healthy foods and work out. What a concept, right? But up until that point I never once considered my health before my never-ending mission to get skinny. I agreed to her novel idea under one condition: that I could still drink (I mean hello, a 20-something working for MTV living in NYC needs her cocktails!) She said yes, but I could only drink champagne. She swore champagne was the lightest drink you could have, clocking in at about 90 calories per glass, and plus, how sexy is a glass of bubbly? Fast forward and I wound up not only losing weight on my new "Champagne Diet", but losing the dead weight in my life: an unhealthy relationship, a job I couldn't stand, and a lot of other negativity in my life at the time. I felt so empowered, so glamorous, and so gorgeous when I held a glass of champagne in my hand and I knew I was onto something. I began to view champagne as a metaphor for my new life and vowed to start celebrating everything. I decided to write a book about my experience but knew I needed a blog to build my platform. I launched TheChampagneDiet.com (long before the Drake song ever existed, just FYI!) It actually kind of bums me out that people use that name all the time for parties and on t-shirts, but I get where it comes from. I actually had to register "The Champagne Diet" trademark because I wanted people to know I owned the name and I was serious about it. So if you're starting out as a blogger, get your legal paperwork straight! You won't regret it.

How did you find your direction and content?

My inspiration comes from my life experiences. You always know what I'm going through because I write about it. I have to, it's my form of therapy and hopefully my readers' too :)

How often do you post?

Not often enough! Ideally I'd love to post once a week, but I find a lot of people now prefer shorter, bite-sized posts on social media, specifically Instagram. I typically "blog" inside of my newsletter now which goes out once a week, and then I transfer those posts over to my website.

Do you think it's important to comment on other blogs?

Absolutely! We have to support each other. I try to do this as often as I can.

Do you use photoshop for graphics or are you graphically challenged?

I use an app called Wordswag for all my photos. I'm obsessed with it!

Was there a moment you felt like "I made it" In terms of your blogs success?

I've been feeling that way a lot recently, especially when I see girls quoting my book and making little photos of my quotes on Instagram. The fact that they take the time to create a shareable piece of art based on inspiration from my writing is kinda mind blowing (and so awesome!)

Is there one particular thing you did that made your blog succeed?

I was consistent! I kept writing and kept sharing my work, even when I saw all these other awesome blogs around me blowing up. You have to believe in yourself and know that as long as you are happy doing what you're doing, you will be successful. I also believe you define success on your own terms, so as long as you feel good about your work, you're a success.

What would you say is the biggest benefit being a "blogger" has given you?

Definitely the ability to connect with and inspire other women. Having a platform is a huge responsibility, but it makes me feel so good to receive emails from my readers telling me something I posted literally changed their lives.

Is your blog used to supplement your business or is your blog your business?

Truth be told, my blog doesn't make me any money. My blog became the launchpad for my writing and coaching career, so if you look at it in the bigger picture my blog contributes to my overall revenue, but I don't do ads or anything like that. It's all a part of my overall brand strategy.

Any advice for any new or novice bloggers?

Don't expect to be an overnight success! All the bloggers you admire have put in YEARS of hard work. It takes consistency, dedication, and a willingness to learn in every situation. Don't be discouraged if your blog doesn't take off right away and don't be obsessed with your followers, etc. They will come. Just keep doing what you love to do.

Chapter 7:

MAKE THAT MONEY HONEY

ONLINE ADVERTISING:
A FEW TERMS YOU SHOULD KNOW...

CPC
(COST PER CLICK)

is the amount paid by an advertiser per click through on an advertisement.

CPM
(COST PER MILLE)

is the amount that it will cost you to have your advertisement shown for 1,000 pageviews.

These are the two most popular forms of advertising. When I first started out advertising on my blog, I learned that most advertising programs will pay you CPM, at an unfixed rate. The more page views you have, the higher your CPM payment rate will be. It's all very intense and a bit confusing, but if you can just grasp the basics of this concept you will be just fine.

GOOGLE ADSENSE
AND OTHER MEDIA PROGRAMS

Despite what most people say, I personally recommend setting up an advertising media program immediately. I had a very good run with Google because I integrated Google Adsense to my blog from the beginning. Google starts your payment rate based on pageviews, so the longer your ads are up and pageviews accumulate, the bigger your account will be in the long run. Don't wait to add Adsense till you are a more established blogger, it will take the same length of time to build up your pageview rankings. It's up to you as to what you will do, but I want to share with you what worked for me. Please, take my advice people!

P.S.

There are various forms of media publishers out there that will want to work with you on your site as it grows. I believe that all of them are mutually beneficial programs, so go for it. BlogHer, GlamMedia, ModernLivingMedia, all very reputable too! You can contact them for more info.

a few words on advertising & sponsors

I have heard a lot of other bloggers that say
very negative things about advertising and sponsored post
on blogs. People think it might turn readers away if you are
just being promotional and not generating true content of
your interest. I strongly disagree. We all need to make money,
so why not get paid for the free promoting that you are
doing for other companies. To be clear, I urge you to only
blog about or endorse products that you truly love
and believe in, don't sell out to make a dollar.
Do what you feel is the right thing and if that is to charge
and put up ads, I say WHY NOT? Like I have said before,
treat your blog like a business and you will most likely be
thrilled with the results.

P.S. Google Ads will only display ads based on what your
readers interests are. They display ads based on the most
recent sites they have been to and what their recent Google
searches are. Google is very smart that way. They won't
display something that the customer isn't interested in already.

GIVEAWAYS ARE GOLDEN

I have been involved in several giveaway opportunities and its such a great exchange of services and for the most part, very mutually beneficial. It involves a post from you reviewing a product or service and enticing your readers to take a look at the product up for grabs.
You can decide the terms of your giveaway however you want that make it beneficial for both parties. I strongly suggest to look at other blogs and see what their terms are and follow suit. It's pretty standard out in blog land and feel free to make it your own, you really can't go wrong!

IN GIVEAWAYS, BE SURE TO INCORPORATE YOUR SOCIAL MEDIA OUTLETS. SPREADING THE WORD ON FACEBOOK, INSTAGRAM, TWITTER , ETC. IS A GREAT WAY TO GET MORE READER EXPOSURE!

SASHA

A FEW CHOICES:
BLOGGER OR WORDPRESS?
WORDPRESS
PINTEREST OR TUMBLR?
I LOVE THEM BOTH!
FACEBOOK OR TWITTER?
TWITTER
PERSONAL OR BUSINESS ONLY?
BOTH!

EVERYTHINGFAB.COM

What inspired you to start your blog?
It's actually not very glam. I had some medical complications with my youngest son and after the treatment I did with him, friends and family started encouraging me to write a book about it. So one day I decided if I was going to tell the story I should start practicing. So i opened a blogger's account , without knowing much about blogging, but every time I sat down to do a post I could't write about the past and what happened... I only wanted to write about things I always loved... fashion, decor, entertaining!

How did you find your direction + content?
Content was easy, fashion, entreating, food and decor has always been my passion. What took sometime to develop was the blog personality, but once I started blogging day in and day out, the style emerged on its own.

How often do you post?.
I try to do at least one post per day plus one weekend post sharing links.

Do you think its important to comment on other blogs?
I think is important to relate and connect with other bloggers, to visit their blogs, send email, tweet, etc. When it comes to commenting, I believe Is not something you need to do all the time or comment on something you don't like but it's great to receive comments so it's nice to give them! I wish I would find more time to comment! I This is such a beautiful community of fabulous ladies & gents that after time you actually end up developing great friendships.

Do you use photoshop for graphics or are you graphically challenged?
I use PSE and Picasa but just the basics. Enough to enhance a picture, add some light and erase or correct something. Would love to learn more!

Was there a moment when you felt an "i made it" moment in terms of your blogs success?
I had a lot of "OMG I can't believe it" moments...like when asked to do a guest post, or an interview or when I have 20+ comments on a post or a special email from a reader. In terms of success I am happy when I feel I can inspire somebody somewhere to do something different; dress with a new accessory, re-decorate a corner in the house, try a new recipe... that is what I strive for every day!

Is there one particular thing you did that helped your blog succeed?
I guess something that helped me, looking back, was to use tumblr to complement my blog and get more exposure to my likes. And actually my tumblr blog has a life of its own. Another things that helped was using as many channels as possible from twitter, interest, alltop, etc.

What would you say is the biggest benefit being a "blogger" has given you?
Wuaw so many! The connection I have made with women through out the world is one of the biggest blessings. It also helped me enjoy my passion of fashion and decor even more and I become much more clear on my likes and dislikes. In a way, thanks to blogging, I developed a stronger sense and acceptance of self. It also kept me current with my profession on how bloggers are changing the PR and marketing game for brands. It really is the gift that keeps on giving...!!

Is your blog used to supplement your business or is your blog your business?
I considered my blog one of my businesses.

Any advice for new or novice bloggers....?
Just go for it wholeheartedly. If you have something to share and you are passionate about it, people will start reading. And enjoy the journey... blogging is really about the journey!!!

Chapter 8:
WORKIN' IT

BRAND IT!

As I mentioned in an earlier chapter, the importance of having a consistent brand for your blog is so crucial to your blog. You want to create a very easily recognizable logo or look, so that people will become increasingly aware of your presence. The more they see your logo, the more familiar they will be with who you are and you can establish that relationship with them. It's all about the psychology of it. You want to create loyal readership and give your readers something tangible that they can relate to.

Now, I am not saying you have to go out and hire a pricey designer to create for you a logo. You could just have the title of your blog in a certain font or color, but whatever you do make sure that you are consistent with it. You may not see the relevance of this in the beginning, but putting this key factor in place before your blog grows will pay off in the end.

The Decorista MY LOGO

MARKETING 101

Once you have established your brand logo and have it on your blog and elsewhere, create business cards and maybe some letterhead. I also recommend adding your logo to the bottom of your email. Having all of these elements working together will give you MAXIMUM effectivity on the marketing end of things. It's all about everything working synergistically.

SYNERGY:

may be defined as two or more things functioning together to produce a result not independently obtainable.

be your own PR girl

PRESS KIT- this is usually a one or two page PDF of the mission statement or reason behind your blog. If you are a business, this can be your one sheet. You want to make sure that you have something to send out to potential readers or businesses just incase they want to know more "about your brand".

PRICE LIST- If you are accepting sponsors or offering advertising put together a PDF with your rates, and your stats including your reader demographic. You can also add any other relevant information that you feel sponsors want to know.

CONTACT LIST- Once you start blogging you will notice that you will be emailing with key people back and forth. I put together a list of my contacts that I feel are great for networking a blogging. This way when you have something to promote, such as a nomination for a contest, or a new business launch you will have a ready-to-go list of people that you can send an email to. (When doing an e-mail blast, be sure to BCC everyone. Otherwise you can have a major disaster on your hands)

NETWORK = POWER

As I have said before, the best way to put your self out there is to get out there and meet people! Do your research and get moving. I didn't get to start my own business by just sitting back and waiting for it to happen. I attended any event in my area, and when there wasn't events, I decided to put them together myself. I saved up money and went on trips to big blogger conventions to help put my brand out there. I emailed back and forth with people who I admired and asked them how they got where they were. Ask someone you admire to lunch to talk "blogging" with, some of my best ideas came after talking with other bloggers. Most importantly, don't ever be afraid to ask questions, most people love answering them!

Entrepreneuress yourself!

When you think of your blog like a business, the sky is the limit in terms of what you can do with it. If you even just devote a small amount of energy to making it a strategic brand and try to grow it, it will grow. I always have known the importance of setting goals for myself. Even if your goal is just to get recognized by a local magazine, then you need to determine the steps it will take to get you there. Go to that magazines events, email the press rep over and over until you hear something back, you get the idea. Remember to be diligent and too much is never enough!

AS THEY SAY...
DRESS FOR THE JOB THAT YOU WANT, NOT THE JOB YOU ALREADY HAVE!

LISA

A FEW CHOICES:
blogger or wordpress?
wordpress
pinterest or tumblr?
pinterest
facebook or twitter?
twitter
personal or business only?
There's a fine line between the two

WITHSTYLE.ME

What inspired you to start your blog?
I was working [endless hours] in the world of advertising when I had a big health scare that landed me in the hospital. Shortly before all that, I had started a blog as a creative outlet; it was my happy place, pulling beautiful content from around the web. As I worked to rebuild my strength I decided it was time to create and share my own content. I [quickly] jumped into the kitchen and began baking and cooking, the two things that I loved to do! My mom offered me her camera, that way I could share my delicious masterpieces with the world and the next thing I knew [1 year later], I was being offered jobs as a food photographer, recipe creator/tester and referred to as the "gluten-free entertaining" expert. With Style and Grace is a lifestyle and food blog, inspiring beauty in everyday lives.

How did you find your direction + content?
If you're passionate about something and you follow [well, listen] to your heart, you'll find your direction. I've always been passionate about food, inspiring and connecting with people. It wasn't until I stopped to listened, often the hardest part, I found my direction and then the content followed.

How often do you post?
I post between 3-4 times a week.

Do you think it's important to comment on other blogs?
Personally, leaving comments on blogs is a way for me to connect with bloggers and a chance to leave a fun "note", as I like to say. I still smile every time I see a new comment on my blog and if I can do that for someone else, perfect!

Do you use photoshop for graphics or are you graphically challenged?
I use it for a few "touch ups", but far from being photoshop savvy.

Was there a moment when you felt an "i made it" moment in terms of your blogs success?
When I got an email requesting to would be a "foodie contributor", that was the turning point. It gave me the confidence which then open my eyes to see that the possibilities were endless!

Is there one particular thing you did that helped your blog succeed?
Connecting with people, face to face, as well as having original content was a part in the success of my blog. I'm all about relationships and having that connection with people is very important to me.

What would you say is the biggest benefit being a "blogger" has given you?
Oh, where do I begin! The people I've met and the relationships created has been the biggest reward, hands down. Within relationships, come possibilities. Blogging is also my creative outlet, a place where I can share my recipes, photographs and inspirations, etc. I think is important for everyone to have – not blogging specific, but any form
[pottery, knitting, painting, etc.].

Is your blog used to supplement your business or is your blog your business?
Currently, I view my blog as a platform for my business.

Chapter 9:

CURATE YOUR LIFE

CLEAN OUT YOUR CLOSET

Like I mentioned in the last chapter, you've got to present yourself in a way that looks like you mean business. As much as your presence matters when you walk into an interview, the way you present yourself in online media is just as important. I encourage you to take this very seriously.

Is your home office, where you will probably be starting your blog, a disaster? If so, clean it up! Is your closet and mess and filled with clothes that are old and ragged? Get rid of them! Get organized and get yourself together before you even begin working on your blog. I promise, you will thank me later. When you are operating from a clean and put together groove, you will flow.

One thing that I can tell you from experience is that the blog + online business world is massive now. So, if you want to bring something different to the table, you have to be ready to play ball. Most of the really successful bloggers are constantly showing pictures of their wardrobes, a peek into their homes, their shoe collections,etc. You don't have to own a Celine bag or Louboutins to have a swoon worthy blog. However, you do have to bring it with style.

You've got to make your bed everyday, keep your clothes nice and clean, take care of your shoes and bags. You want your desk to free of clutter, and why not the rest of your home while you are at it. Organize things to look nice and presentable in photos. Buy yourself flowers every once and while, get really good smelling candles. Take care of yourself the way you would want the world to see that you do.

THE CREATIVE FLOW

Even if you aren't the most creative gem on the planet, that's cool, blogging is for you too. You're going to need to get your home and life in order to set yourself up for successfully building and blog and brand that lasts.

Once your home is tidy and organized, I want to encourage you to create an inspiring space for yourself to get in the creativity zone. Because, more often than not, you will get in a creative block where you feel uninspired and not wanting to commit to your blog.

I like to call this my version of "DECOR THERAPY".
Here are a few things to do to get your blog space ready for your flow.

1. Create a vision board/ inspiration board and put it in your office. Include images you want to evoke feelings of or words that give you a burst of energy.
2. Create a sanctuary area where you can take a few deep breaths and meditate before you get to work. Clear out your mind in a cozy chair that makes you feel safe and inspired. Do this before every blogging session.
3. Get energizing candles that smell delicious. Create a habit of lighting the candle every time you write a blog post. Make the ritual fun and exciting each time you do it.
4. Set up small areas of your home that you style for photos. You can totally take it down after the photo, but constantly use the area in your home to create inspiring vignettes. Maybe use your dining table decor as constantly rotating content for blog posts. Or try re organizing a bookcase every week for a style segment, your closet can have endless inspired looks.

THE BENEFITS OF
VLOGGING

. . . .

Once your home is tidy and organized, I want to encourage you to create an inspiring space for yourself to get in the creativity zone. Because, more often than not, you will get in a creative block where you feel uninspired and not wanting to commit to your blog. Therefore, using your style and decor skills will really come into play. You've got to make sure that your surroundings reflect what is going on inside of your soul.

In the famous words of Coco Chanel
"An interior is the natural projection of the soul."

This will also lend as a backdrop if you decide to add video blogging to your blog. A YouTube channel is a FANTASTIC way to get exposure and a new following fast. So many people are on the YouTube pathway. You can add each of the elements we talked about in earlier chapters to your YouTube blog. You will have a space to add keywords, Google Adsense, newsletter sign ups, etc. I highly suggest doing this weather you are just starting out your blog or have been blogging for a while. It's new new thing that gets massive responses.

So get to decorating your space!
Need some inspiration? Visit my blog
www.thedecorista.com

a few last words...

Blogging has single handedly changed my life. It has taken me on a road that I never even imagined and I know that it has done the same for many of my counterparts, too! It has allowed me to fulfill my passion in life, meet incredibly amazing and talented people, have relationships with readers all over the world. What an incredible blessing, no?

Whether you are already a blogger or you are just starting out, I want to encourage you that no idea is too small and no dream is too big. I promise that if you implement the information that I have given you, you can be successful! You may not end up where you thought you would, but that is the joy of the journey. My journey went from desperately seeking any job within the design world, and now I am not only running my very own interior design business in New York City, some people consider me a design influencer (i mean...seriously???) With a lot of hard work, persistence and a vision, I made my own way. It is incredibly empowering to know that I did it myself from basically nothing, and I believe in my heart of hearts that if I did it, you can do it too!

FOLLOW YOUR DREAMS JELLYBEANS!

xoxo

Resources

SOCIAL MEDIA SITES

FACEBOOK.COM
TWITTER.COM
INSTAGRAM.COM
PINTEREST.COM
LINKEDIN.COM
BLOGGER.COM
BLOGHER.COM
BLOGLOVIN.COM
BLOGRANKINGS.COM
MASHABLE.COM
TECHNORATI.COM
BLOGTOPSITES.COM
BLOGGED.COM
FRIENDFEED.COM
STUMBLEUPON.COM
REDDIT.COM

BLOG HOSTS

SQUARESPACE.COM
BLOGGER.COM
WORDPRESS.COM
TYPEPAD.COM
LIVEJOURNAL.COM
XANGA.COM
WEEBLY.COM

GRAPHICS

FLICKR.COM
CANVA.COM
PHOTOBUCKET.COM
PICASA.COM
PICNIK.COM
PIXIR.COM

PROGRAMS

MAC PAGES 09'
PHOTOSHOP ELEMENTS

AFFILIATE OPTIONS

SHARE A SALE
REWARD STYLE
THINGLINK

RESCOURCES TO FOR MORE OF MY ADVICE + HELP

WWW.THEDECORISTA.COM
E-COURSES:
UNLEASH YOUR ISTA + THE PAID DECORATOR

The End

NOTES:

www.ingramcontent.com/pod-product-compliance
Lightning Source LLC
Chambersburg PA
CBHW041430050326
40690CB00002B/492